FORUM FOR SOCIAL STUDIES (FSS)

FSS Studies on Poverty No. 3

Destitution in the North-Eastern Highlands of Ethiopia

Community and Household Studies in Wag Hamra and South Wello

By

Yared Amare

Addis Ababa
Forum for Social Studies
August 2003

ISBN: 1-904855-71-7

ISBN-13: 978-1-904855-71-2

Layout by: Mihret Demissew

Table of Contents

Abstract

Rural destitution is a growing phenomenon in Ethiopia, closely associated with population growth, resource scarcity, crop failure and famine. This paper attempts to further our understanding of destitution by discussing its attributes, local developments that contextualize it, and the causes and processes which explain why certain households fall into or emerge from a state of destitution. The study was conducted in a woina dega community in Wag Hamra zone and a kola community in South Wello. The research methods used in the study consisted of group interviews with men and women and household case studies.

Important aspects of the socio-economic context that condition the distribution of destitution include the occurrence of droughts, the variable impact of land redistribution, other mechanisms of gaining land and development interventions, declining trends in resource availability, and ecological and living conditions. The discussion of the causes and processes of destitution demonstrates the role of severe or repeated crop failure, poor access to assets and the social development of households in bringing about destitution. The resilience of households that manage to avoid destitution despite experiencing various hazards lie in their substantial assets, diversification activities and social networks. On the other hand, households that are reduced to destitution have to rely on limited income-earning activities and support from other community members to survive. Some households do manage to escape destitution on the basis of successful investments in crop and livestock production, efforts to diversify their income sources, and resource donations from kin and friends. Favorable conditions including access to key assets such as land, labor or reproductive animals have to be available to households if this is going to be likely. Development interventions such as credit provision for seed, animals and income-earning activity, road building and those promoting urban growth have had some impact in allowing households to avoid impoverishment. Finally the paper argues that that fight against destitution and poverty in the Ethiopian highlands should integrate four vital strategies: an anti-drought/famine strategy, an agricultural strategy, an income diversification strategy and a demographic strategy.

1

Destitution in the North-Eastern Highlands of Ethiopia
Community and Household Studies in Wag Hamra and South Wello

Yared Amare

Introduction

It has become apparent that due to population growth and land degradation, crop and market failures associated with droughts and other environmental factors, as well as low access to assets, the prevalence of poverty and destitution has reached unacceptably high levels in Ethiopia. An estimated 47.5% of all rural households are thought to be poor, whereas 13.8% of households in the Northeastern Highlands are estimated to be destitute (MEDAC 2002; Devereux, Sharp and Yared 2002). Although the broader parameters of poverty and destitution are well known, the multiple and inter-linked ways in which individual households fall into and out of poverty and destitution are less well understood.

This paper discusses the nature and processes of destitution experienced by households in two communities of Wag Hamra and South Wello zones. It utilizes qualitative data from group interviews and household case studies including life histories that were used to document people's perceptions and experiences of destitution. The data for this paper was collected as part of the study entitled 'Destitution in Ethiopia's North-Eastern Highlands', a collaborative study between the Institute of Development Studies at Sussex University and Save the Children, UK, Ethiopia (Devereux, Sharp and Yared 2002).

In this research project, destitution was defined as a state of extreme poverty in which households cannot meet their basic needs, lacked access to the productive assets that were necessary to escape poverty, and were dependent on formal or informal resource transfers (Swift 1989; Devereux, Sharp & Yared 2002). Destitution may be a long term state of severe poverty and deprivation caused by lack of access to basic assets such as land (Dasgupta 1993; Dessalegn 2002). It also occurs suddenly as an integral part of livelihood shocks such as famine and a prerequisite for mass starvation and deaths (Walker 1989:143). Such attributes of destitution are obviously highly relevant in the Ethiopian context.

The above definition of destitution and peasant self-assessments of livelihood status were used to combine variables from the study survey to come up with a composite index of destitution. On the basis of this index, 13.8% of households in North and South Wello and Wag Hamra zones were estimated to be destitute, which constitutes 564,426 people out of an estimated population of around 4,000,000 in the three zones (Devereux, Sharp & Yared 2002). Using data on the growing frequency of famines, declining food

1

consumption and increasing malnutrition, Dessalegn has argued that the proportion of destitute households in Ethiopia has increased substantially over the past half century (Dessalegn 2002). This is supported by peasant subjective assessments which attest to the same trend (Aklilu and Dessalegn 2001; Devereux, Sharp & Yared 2002).

Apart from the large number of destitute households, the concept of destitution has an even more important significance. Destitution not only represents an extreme form of food-insecurity, poverty and vulnerability, but goes further because it also highlights how and why households become susceptible to them. Destitution therefore not only signifies an outcome in terms of welfare and capabilities, but is also useful in illuminating processes of impoverishment (Devereux, Sharp & Yared 2002). A process approach is important because destitution is a complex phenomenon that results from a varying combination of events and causes, affecting households of variable vulnerability to produce different trajectories towards it (Yared 2002).

The paper starts out by describing community perspectives on the nature and causes of destitution to throw light on its local significance. Subsequently, the paper discusses contextual factors such as the occurrence of drought, land redistributions, trends in local ecology and livelihood conditions, as well as the impact of development interventions, that condition patterns of destitution. Household case studies are used to examine how and why households fall into, cope with and emerge from destitution. Household experiences of processes of destitution show how environmental and social factors, resource access, idiosyncratic events and livelihood strategies interact to produce distinctive routes into destitution. The paper also shows how such processes of destitution result in the emergence of different types of destitutes who are differentiated by varying mixtures of asset deficits. Despite the occurrence of factors and events that undermine their viability, households are able to exert successful strategies that prevent their fall into destitution. The paper discusses particular mixes of strategies and asset requirements that make this possible. On the other hand, it also shows how households who fail to avoid destitution make use of a variety of coping mechanisms and networks of social support to try to meet their consumption deficits and survive from year to year. Some households do manage to escape destitution, and some of the typical strategies, asset requirements and conditions that make this possible are discussed.

The Study Areas

The data on which this paper is based was collected in two of the nine sites in which the qualitative part of the study was carried out. The first site was the *got* of Adi Maya in the *woina dega kebele* of Addis Alem, which was located in Sekota Wereda of Wag Hamra zone. In Adi Maya, households had landholdings averaging 3 timad (approximately .75 ha) in size, on which they grew barely, wheat, beans, peas, teff, sorghum, lentils, flax, safflower, chickpeas and millet. The second site was the *got* of Aya Ager in the lowland *kebele* of Kolegna, located in Kalu *wereda* of South Wollo. The size of the landholdings in this area ranged from 1 to 6 timad (.25 ha to 1.5 ha), and farmers mainly grew sorghum, teff and maize, but also haricot beans, sesame and chickpeas to a limited extent.

Methodology

Group interviews were conducted with several groups of men and women in both research sites to collect data on community perspectives on the nature and context of destitution, including characteristics and living conditions of the destitute and the role of climatic factors, land redistributions, resource scarcity and development interventions in patterning destitution.

The household case studies were used to collect in-depth data on the processes by which individual households fell into and out of destitution. The case studies were expected to provide concrete data on the actual experiences of households. This is important because specific household attributes, their individual strategies, covariation in the occurrence of events and local contexts rather than the occurrence of specific events determined the status of household livelihoods.

The case studies collected data on the multiple facets of household livelihoods that determined whether they fell into, escaped or avoided destitution. These facets included the means and levels of resource access, sequences of events and trends in the economic status of households, livelihood strategies, the role of social institutions and exchange mechanisms and the impact of development interventions.

Household case studies were carried out with household heads from different age and gender categories who were interviewed for about 2 to 3 hours on these issues. Households were selected purposively to include destitutes, those who had emerged from destitution, and well-off households in order to gain a varied perspective into the determinants of destitution (see annex).

Community Perceptions of Destitution[1]

Group interviews carried out in the two study communities revealed that there were certain households who were thought to belong to a category that could be described as destitute. Various terms were used to refer to this category such as *deha* and *chigeregnoch*. They were thought to be short of food for a substantial part of the year, mainly due to lack or shortage of land, livestock and farming equipment that they could use to maintain a certain level of productivity. Due to lack of labor and draft power, they were often forced to rent out their land. Their houses were often in poor condition and unable to protect them from the elements because they did not have the means to conduct repairs. Their clothing was often in poor condition since they were able to buy only once in several years. The types of people who were likely to become destitute were female heads of households, the elderly and the landless.

---

[1] The sections on community perceptions and context of destitution are products of collaborative work by the author and Dejene Negassa.

In order to survive from year to year, they had to supplement their income by selling wood, charcoal, rope and handicrafts, and engaging in wage labor. They also consumed cabbage and other wild plants, and rationed food in the pre-harvest season.

The main causes of destitution were thought to be crop failure due to drought and other crop hazards, as well as lack of land which led to the distress sale of livestock. Population growth was thought to be the factor behind land shortages experienced by community members. Individual characteristics such as laziness, extended illness and wastefulness were also perceived to cause destitution in some cases. Poor people were also often indebted to others at interests rates as high as 100 percent, which was likely to throw them into or keep them in destitution.

The Context of Destitution

Drought

Droughts, which occurred at variable frequencies and with variable impact in different areas of the region, brought about the death and crises sale of livestock that impoverished many households. The drought which occurred around 1984-85 (of variable duration in different regions) is generally seen as the most destructive in terms of the loss of livelihoods and mortality. This drought had a prolonged impact for many people because post-drought recovery was made difficult by survivors' physical weakness and the lack of oxen and seed which was sometimes not addressed by post-recovery interventions. Very little was done to prevent the loss of animals before they died.

The duration of self-provisioning of food is declining as well. While better off households are able to acquire grain on the market by selling livestock, other households have been forced to resort to the sale of firewood or charcoal or migrate for wage labour in other regions.

Land Redistribution

The land redistributions of the EPRDF conducted in the early 1980s in much of the study area significantly defined patterns of access to land that were highly relevant to destitution processes. The EPRDF land redistributions, which were far-reaching in nature, divided all the land in one kebele into categories of fertility and proximity to residences and allocated land individually to all males above the age of 24 and females above 18. While this led to relatively equal access to land in the community and made land available to the marginalized, such as female household heads and the youth, households which fared less well in the lotteries and who were not favored by corrupt officials, young people who were not old enough to be eligible for land allocations during the redistribution and returnees from resettlement had relatively less access to land which enhanced their vulnerability to destitution. Whereas households who received fertile land benefited from the higher productivity and lower seed requirements of their land, those who happened to get infertile plots of land were much less productive and less able to have the surplus they could invest in assets. The fact that family size was not considered in the allocation was also likely to bring about inequity in access to land. Reductions of 'their husband's 'share of land from widows also exacerbated the impact of their loss of male labor and impoverished them. Some young people were able to receive land from their parents as marriage endowments or inheritance, but variations in parental landholdings meant that they received variable amounts of land in such a manner. Many young households were therefore dependent on the land market for access to land, but their limited access to oxen and seed meant they were at a disadvantage in the competition to get land on the market.

Other outcomes of the land redistribution such as the relative homogenization of landholdings also had the effect of extending land shortages over a larger proportion of households, which, combined with its role in reducing fertility maintenance, farming practices such as fallowing and crop rotation, was perceived to have an adverse impact on agricultural productivity. Inequitable demarcation of land between kebeles that was thought to have occurred sometimes was likely to reduce land access in some kebeles as well.

The land market is also changing, partly as a result of the land redistributions, and in a way that has some implications for destitution processes. Growing land scarcity is responsible for shifting the terms of land transactions towards landlords, often poor farmers who are forced to put their land on the market for lack of inputs such as oxen, labor and seed. Thus, changes such as the terms of sharecropping arrangements shifting to equal shares between landlord and rentor and the elimination of compensation for seed inputs to the rentor have occurred. In addition, cash rentals of land which are favored by landlords are expanding at the expense of sharecropping arrangements. This puts households with greater cash resources at an advantage in comparison to others. All this has reduced the benefits that households who are landless or short of land could derive from the land market, thereby weakening their ability to fight-off destitution.

Trends in local ecology and livelihoods

An important overall trend is the increase in land scarcity associated with population growth. This has meant not only a decline in the amount of land available to households but also a decline in the fertility of land because the limited size of landholdings limit the scope for fertility maintenance activities such as fallowing and crop rotation. Land scarcity has also led to a decrease in household livestock holdings due to reduced availability of grazing land and animal feed. Households are also having to put in more labor in plowing their land repeatedly in order to secure a certain level of production from smaller and less fertile landholdings. Households that are less able to meet these higher labor demands are less productive or have to rent out their land both of which erode their income and asset base.

Environmental and agricultural conditions are perceived to have declined since the 1984-85 drought, mainly due to lower and erratic rainfall but also the growing incidence of pests and weeds. This has meant deteriorating crop performance and overall impoverishment of communities. There are now virtually no wealthy peasants who can loan money to households in need. For the same reason, employment opportunities on local farms, which are important sources of income for poor households, have declined as well. Farmers have responded to the growing problems of low rainfall, pests and weeds by altering the crop varieties they plant towards varieties that may be lower in yield levels as well as price on the market.

All this has also resulted in a lower capacity for food self-provisioning by households, which has in turn led to greater reliance on more frequently occurring markets to acquire grains, as well as increased labor migration which has gained further impetus by the impact of the 1984-85 drought, the resettlement efforts and the land redistribution of the early 1980s.

There is a general perception that the living conditions and asset base of young people compares poorly with that of their parents at the same age. Young people start off their marriage with less because their parents who are poorer than in previous days provide them with less resources as marriage endowments or inheritance.

Development Interventions

There are a number of interventions carried out by government and NGOs in local communities. One of these, the extension package that makes fertilizer and seed available to farmers, has been variably successful. While it has increased yield in some areas, the risk of crop loss due to lack of rain and other reasons has resulted in financial loss and indebtedness for a substantial proportion of households. There are programs which provide credit for the purposes of acquiring oxen and sheep and engaging in other income earning activities. While these have been beneficial, their potential has been restricted by low availability of credit, risk associated with the loss of animals and inappropriate timing of credit disbursement and repayment vis-à-vis prices of cattle on the market. Transactions in informal credit are less prevalent, especially since the 1984-85 famine, due to the fact that the number of people who are able to give credit or to take the high interest credit available on the informal market has declined.

Employment schemes such as EGS and food-for-work, provide income to a substantial number of households. There are reservations regarding the use of group labor to construct terraces that is seen as too demanding for the payment given. Terraces are also sometimes disapproved of for fragmenting plots, removing topsoil for their construction which is washed away when they are broken, and as breeding places for rats that destroy crops. The construction of roads under these schemes is generally looked upon more favorably for its positive impact on grain availability and prices in local markets as well as accessibility to food aid. There were similar views regarding irrigation works which were seen to allow farmers to diversify their crops and engage in multiple cropping.

Processes of Destitution

Destitution is a complex process that occurs as a result of a variable number and combination of events. This is because households are characterized by different asset levels, demographic and social characteristics, and social and economic contexts. Most apparently, destitution commonly appears to be caused by crop failure that occurs due to the frequent droughts or rain failures as well as other hazards such as pests, hailstorm, excessive rain and frost. Households respond by selling their assets often cheaply to buy grain, thereby ending up in destitution. The experiences of Muhaili, a middle aged farmer, are illustrative:

> *I spent my early childhood in my grandparent's house. I then started to work as a servant for many years. I had been to able to acquire two oxen, when I rejoined my parent's household in order to help them out as they were facing food shortages in 1984/85. I sold the oxen for 200 Birr each to buy food for the joint household. My parents also became sick at the time. We all had to go to Asosa (a resettlement locality), including my sister, and brother who died there.*

While some households become destitute due to a single crop failure, repeated crop failures have to occur before more resilient households are reduced to a similar state (Goyder and Goyder 1988; Swift 1989). For instance, although crop failure impoverished Nurtoyar's household by greatly diminishing their assets, he did manage to avoid total destitution because of his assets were substantial initially, some of which he was able to sell while preserving others.

> *In 1984/85, a crop disease in addition to drought destroyed the sorghum. We replanted the land with teff in August but it failed because of the drought. By this year, our livestock holdings had grown to 2 oxen, 2 bulls and 2 cows. That year, we sold all our livestock for as much as 200 birr per ox, and were left with 1 calf, 1 ox and 1 goat. We survived by eating what was left of the sorghum and wild plants including some types of leaves and wood, and weeds mixed with grain, and also received 2 sacks of food aid every 2 months. We became very weak that year.*

A common and related outcome is the prospect of continued destitution when households who lack draft oxen or seed are forced to sharecrop out their land. Not only would they have lost assets but they are also forced to take up asset degrading strategies that hampers theirs productivity in a way that exacerbates and perpetuates their destitution. Tadele's testimony illustrates this outcome:

> *Our crops failed partially in 1983/84 and we got only 5 quintals. I had 2 children in town and 5 children here at the time. I had to sell my two oxen that year. I cultivated my land, exchanging my labor for oxen, but the crops failed totally. I was also sick from August to Tikemt. We therefore left for the relief camps in Korem. We left some of our land fallow and sharecropped out the rest for a third of the output which amounted to 4.5 quintals, due to lack of seed and draft power. We left some of our land fallow and sharecropped out the rest for a third of the output which amounted to 4.5 quintals, due to lack of seed and draft power..... I had no*

> *cattle to lose that year. I rented out all of my bereha land for 50% of the output for lack of seed, and planted the wejed, exchanging my labor for oxen. I have been renting out my land since.... I divorced my wife in 1997 because we disagreed over how she was managing our grain stocks. She was wasteful which was part of the reason behind our decline... I also had saved up 1.5 quintals of lentils from land that I had rented in, which I intended to use to buy an ox, but it was stolen in my absence. I would have been able to get my land back if I had been able to get an ox.*

As Tadele explained, his impoverishment was worsened by a 'wasteful' wife and the theft of his grain stocks which he had intended to sell to acquire draft power. Thus, other events may compound the effect of crop failure and loss of draft power to intensify the state of impoverishment households find themselves facing.

It is apparent that the landholdings of many households are severely deficient. This may arise from a limited inheritance or failure to receive enough land during local land redistributions. Inadequate landholdings, in conjunction with crop failure, are another important source of destitution for numerous households. The experiences of Moges, a middle-aged farmer, exhibit the compounded effect of the reductions in his family's landholdings implemented by local officials, repeated crop failure and forced sale of oxen, and the resultant need to sharecrop or fallow his land, in impoverishing his household. The process of destitution that he underwent was extended and caused by multiple and inter-linked factors.

> *We built our own house 4 years after we got married. Our living conditions were fair until 1972 when both of my parents died in a single month. Their assets were divided among five siblings. I got only 3 beehives. Part of their landholdings was taken by the kebele as motekeda (the land share of the dead alienated for redistribution) and I was left with only 2 timad of land. We began to fall short because the land was not enough for our needs. The crops also failed in 1983/84, and we left for the camps in Korem....... We planted our land using mekenajo – oxen sharing arrangement – and seed that we bought after selling the ox, but the crops failed completely in 1984/85 as well. We therefore went to Belesa in October to work harvesting crops, leaving our ox with relatives in the dega area..... Our ox died, and we sharecropped our land to two of my brothers for half of the output. I have become poor since 1984/85, due to the death of our oxen and lack of seed..... We sharecropped out our land again the following year, but the crops failed due to drought and damage caused by rats..... We have remained short of food because we have been surviving on 1 quintal of grain a year that we receive from sharecroppers and income from wood and dung sales.*

Some households appear fated for destitution because they had very poor access to key productive resources such as land, oxen and sometimes labor from the time they were formed. This was true in the case of Mohammed Yimer, who had returned from the region of Shewa where he and his brother had been working as migrant laborers having saved enough money to buy one bull each. He appears to have missed the land redistribution and was therefore not able to claim land of his own. The fact that he sold his bull to cover the costs of his wedding and the small size of the land he had access to, relegated him to a state of destitution that he was not able to escape from for a long time.

> *We begged for draft power that year till ours matured. I started to plow 4 timad of my father's land, giving him half of the output. I then got married but my wife did not bring any assets. I sold my ox to cover the expenses of the wedding and continued to use my brother's, which had now become a pair. I brought an ox in a yegerafi arrangement in order to reduce the burden on him. We used to get about 3 quintals that we shared equally with my parents. The grain we get, i.e. 1.5 quintals, was only enough for 3 months even after rationing by eating only 1 injera per person a day. I have also been sharecropping-in some of my uncle's land, getting from 1 to 2 quintals. The total amount of grain we get only lasts seven months. I have not been able to rent more land because of lack of seed and labor for weeding. Land for rent is available in adjacent gots, but not in ours. This year, my father gave me 2 timad out of his 4 timad, leaving 2 timad for his son and himself. The land is stony and unproductive.*

Alemnesh who did not get a proper marriage because of her parents' death never received livestock or had access to enough labor to cultivate the land she inherited, and was therefore destined for destitution from the outset.

> *My parent's died in the early eighties and my brother and I inherited their land, which amounted to 4 timad. He left for Korem during the 1984/85 famine and was never heard from. I did not get any animals from my parents because they died soon after. I started to rent out the land...... I continued to rent out land until the 1990 land redistribution, when I received only 2 timad of infertile bereha land and 1 timad of wejed. I sharecropped out the land for a third of the produce to two young men who had not received any land. I used to get 1 quintal of barley, 1 quintal of sorghum or 1.5 quintal of wheat. The grain runs out around April, so I have to sell dung and wood every 3 to 4 days, until the rainy season. We then subsist on melons and kale that we plant in the backyard as well as injera once in a while.*

Just as the death of his parents initiated a process of decline in the case of Moges outlined above, various events associated with people's lifecycles or households' social development can bring about an attrition of assets that with or without the effect of other elements can cause destitution (McCann 1987; Yared 2002). These developments include an early phase in the establishment of the household, divorce or even feasts for weddings or commemorations that require substantial outlays, old age and the passing away of household heads. For instance, Amemoye, an old female head of household, who was destitute and greatly dependent on her son, narrated these events which first threw her into destitution.

> *I was raised by my mother after my father died as a child. We grew up in poverty, with 2 of my brothers. I got married as an older teenager to a man who had 2 oxen. We lived well, producing 10 quintals. I had 3 children before he died six years after we got married. We subsequently became poor, sold the oxen and sharecropped the land. I raised the children by myself and married-off two of them. I then remarried after a long time but he got sick died after 5 years in 1984/85. I did have a daughter with him. Our living conditions did not improve since he did not have much. I had been given a cow by my son-in-law, which gave me a heifer and a bull, but they all died in 1984/85. I therefore went to the resettlement areas in Asosa, taking 3 children with me.*

It appears that it was the death of her husband and the associated loss of his labor and management skills or the expenses on his funeral that impoverished her household initially by forcing them to sell their oxen and sharecrop out their land. This was followed by the impact of the 1984/85 famine, which pushed her back into destitution after she began to regain some of her assets, by bringing about the death of her second husband and her livestock, forcing her to join a resettlement camp in Western Ethiopia.

In addition to socio-economic occurrences that affect many households at the same time, idiosyncratic events that affect individual households or individuals such as illnesses, accidents or deaths also impoverish them, occurrences which may be compounded by other events as well. This appears to have been true in the case of Beyu, 70, who due to the unfortunate deaths of her four children and a severe physical disability, has not been able to sustain a viable marriage and therefore has been relegated to a prolonged state of destitution and dependency on her sister. It was the idiosyncratic events that she experienced combined with their social implications that appear to have thrown Beyu into a downward spiral of impoverishment from which she could not extricate herself.

> *I was born and got married here in this kebele. For six years, we were living well with my husband who came here from another locality. We had a pair of oxen but he used to have his land plowed for him in his natal kebele. I had four children who all died, so he left me without leaving me anything. I then began to live with my sister. I have had a bad leg since I was a child so I was not able to remarry for another 5 years. I then married an elderly man who had only 3 timad of land which we sharecropped out. We remained in poverty so we got divorced. I therefore started to live with my sister again. We survived the 1984/85 famine together.*

Types of Destitute Households

Such processes of destitution lead to types of destitute households that have distinctively different social and economic characteristics and capabilities. The following presents a typology of destitute households that emerge from the household case studies.

1. Landless/Land-short/Labor adequate/Oxenless Households

Such households remain destitute primarily due to the small size or infertility of the land that they hold. This puts a severe limit on their productivity, which not only results in food-insecurity and lack of income, but also denies them the surplus they can invest on assets such as oxen. Because they have enough labor though, they are able to engage in some types of non-agricultural activity that allows them to earn some income.

Shambel Muhe. Age 24. Family size 9. 7 children. Years of marriage 25. Informant is oldest son in the household.

> *The crops failed in 1984/85 and we left for Harbu to receive food aid. We soon went to my mother's original community which was abandoned by most of the residents, with 7 to 8 livestock and about 16 goats. We gradually sold or slaughtered all of the animals for food.... The following year, we bought seed and planted about 7 timad of land that belonged to people that had been resettled. My father had been given an ox in a yegerafi arrangement to somebody who sold it off but later repaid him. We plowed sharing our ox with others (mekenajo) until we got enough for one more ox. We cultivated the land for three years after which we gave it up when it owners returned from the resettlement areas. We sold one ox, after which we started to trade in goat skins, buying them at Debe (a market 3 to 4 hours away) for sale in the local market of Adame. It was not very profitable. Our remaining ox got sick and was sold for 300 birr to buy food.*
>
> *My uncle had given us .75 timad of land that my mother had inherited, when we came back to this area. We requested draft power from others and hand dug the rest of the land to get fresh maize and 2 quintals of sorghum. We make ends meet by trading goat skins.... We survive by rationing our food, especially in July and August..... I work in neighbouring kebeles in October and November, harvesting teff to buy clothes for myself and my sisters. We also work in the Employment Generation Schemes every year.*

2. Landless/Land-short/Labor-short/Oxenless Households

These households do not only lack adequate amounts of land but also enough labor, especially male labor. This prevents them from making full use of even the small amounts of land they may have, often forcing them to rent out the land. Their lack of land and labor virtually eliminates their possibilities of attaining food security, adequate income or productive assets.

Female-Headed Households

The case of Alemenesh Yalew, a 40 year old female head of household that has already been narrated above is illustrative of households that lack both land and labour. Initially, Alemenesh had sufficient land but due to lack of labour, she rented the land. But the land redistribution of 1990 left her not only with 2 timads of land but 1 timad of infertile bereha land and 1 timad of wejed. She had to sharecrop out the land and received small amount of grain that failed to cover her annual food security requirements. Shse was therefore forced to engage in petty trade and to alter her diet.

Elderly-Headed Households

Age and disability are other factors that aggravate the process of destitution as already observed in the case of Beyu Belachew, a 70 year old disabled and divorced women whose life trajectory was discussed above. Beyu lost four children and was divorced by her first husband. She remarried an elderly man but was divorced again and returned to his previous life with her sister. Beyu and her sister devised livelihood strategies that revolved around petty trade. But age related constraints and her childlessness as well as constraints related to environmental degradation severely limit her life options and push her further into severe forms of destitution.

3. Land owner/Labor Adequate/Capital (seed, ox) Deficient Households

Such households have adequate land and labor but do not have production inputs such as oxen and seed usually because they have previously sustained production failure that has led to loss of assets. This in turn may often force them to sharecrop out their land, which means that their grain supplies are substantially reduced and their ability to acquire assets diminished. The case of Muhaili Merai, who is 45 years of age and whose family size consists of 8 people sex of whom were her children and whose life trajectory has been narrated above is a good case in point. As noted, Muhaili was forced to sell two oxen's during the 1984/85 food shortage. He and his family were subsequently resettled in Asosa but only stayed for two years. On his return to his previous locality he was once again faced with crop failure and forced to sell his ox. Although his landholding is sufficient for his needs the lack of oxen is a major constraint.

Poor or Constrained Households

1. Land short/Labor adequate/Oxen owning Households

Although these households have more or less sufficient access to labor and draft power, their small and infertile landholdings prevent them from attaining food and economic security. They are not destitute but barely manage to make it from year to year.

i. Wondimu G/Michael. Family size – 3. 1 child. 1st marriage – 6 years.

> *I got married in 1995. I was given a bull and a third of their annual grain output by my parents, and my wife brought a heifer….. I had 2 timads of infertile land on the hillside, from which I got 3 quintals of barley and beans or average. My wife was too young to receive land in her name. I have never had small sheep or goats, because we have not had enough to invest in them and there are no people who want to give them out as rebi. The cow had a calf but I sold it last year after our crops partly failed. Our main problem is land shortage. Our normal production keeps us going till April, after which we sell dung and wood every 2 to 3 weeks.…*

ii. Mohammed Yimer. Age –37. Family size – 5. 3 children. 1st marriage

> *The crops failed in 1984/85 when I was only 16….. I refused to be resettled however….. I then went to Jewaha (Shewa) with my brother – where we worked as household laborers for three years. We were able to save enough to buy a bull each…. I started to plow 4 timad of my father's land, giving him half of the output. I then got married but my wife did not bring any assets. I sold my ox to cover the expenses of the wedding and continued to use my brother's which had now become a pair. I brought an ox in a yegerafi arrangement in order to reduce the burden on him. We used to get about 3 quintals that we shared equally with my parents……. This year, my father gave me 2 timad out of his 4 timad, leaving 2 timad for his son and himself. The land is stony and unproductive…..*

2. Land short/Labor-short/Oxen owning Households.

This is an unusual category of households that despite their inadequate landholdings and lack of adequate labor manage to preserve some access to draft power which they rent to supplement their income and grain supplies. However, they still remain food-insecure, having to engage in low profit activities to meet their annual food deficit.

Zenitu Muhe Seid. Age 40. Family size 4. Widow for 7 years after 26 years of marriage.

> *I got married when I was 13, without receiving any assets from my parents…… We were given land by the kebele but we did not farm it much*

because it was not of good quality. We did not have livestock of our own. We lived together for six years, after which crops failed completely due to drought and worms. We went to Harbu to get food aid. After 15 days we volunteered to be resettled in Asosa, Western Ethiopia.....We came back the following year..... We bought two calves with the money we had saved from Asosa. Our land had been taken, so we got a share of his father's land which amounted to 1.5 timad. We lived in difficulty because the land was small and I begged for draft power because my husband remained sick. We only got about 3 quintals of grain from the land which we supplemented with 75 kgs of grain from food aid...... My husband died three to four years later. By then the two calves had grown into 2 oxen. We rented them out for 1.5 quintals each, but the rentors refused to pay the rent when the crops failed. So we get paid only once in a while....... Last year, I got 2 quintals from renting out the oxen and 2 quintals from our own land. We survived by selling wood every week for salt and shire, and also selling goats.

Strategies Used to Combat Destitution

The likelihood of a household falling into destitution is not only dependent on the conjunction of adversities that confront it but also the strategies that it uses to combat processes of destitution (Dessalegn 1991; Yared 2002). The success of these strategies is determined by the specific attributes of households which determine the types of strategies used by them, their capabilities and the opportunities available to them in the local context. One of the strategies that households use to avoid destitution consists of diversification of their income (Webb 1992; Ellis 2000). The following is an instance of how a middle-aged farmer named Abebaw diversified into trading activities in order to survive the impact of crop failures associated with droughts.

Our crops failed completely in 1984/85 due to drought. I did not have to migrate as other people in our kebele however. In order to survive, I traded grain, traveling as far away as Belesa (a woreda in the adjacent zone of North Gonder), using my father's 4 mules..... Most of our livestock died however, 10 of my father's and 3 of mine. He was left with 10 goats and I was left with only a calf. We were not able to find buyers for our livestock in the markets where oxen were being sold at 30 Birr each. In 1985/86, my father and I joined our oxen, bought seed using some of the money I got from trading and planted teff, barley and sorghum on 3 plots of land left uncultivated by other people who had migrated..... We were also able to buy 2 oxen for 130 Birr each that year using income from goat sales and the profit from trading grain.

Although the drought led to the loss of much of his livestock holdings, his ability to engage in grain trading allowed him to acquire food and survive during the difficult period, while retaining the remnants of his livestock assets. He was also able to use the income he derived to purchase inputs and draft oxen that allowed him to reverse the processes of destitution. The fact that he was able to access his father's mules for trading purposes and his familiarity with the activity was a prerequisite for the success of this strategy.

Since non-agricultural activities are often less profitable and unreliable however, many households use a combination of agricultural and non-agricultural activities to fight-off destitution. Nurtoyar, who was shown to face destitution due to repeated crop failure, used a variety of strategies to maintain his livelihood.

> *We planted some land the following year in a mekenajo arrangement with my brother..... We sold goats to buy late maturing sorghum seed..... My wife returned and began to sell charcoal because our output was not enough for a family of six. We sharecropped land and rented an ox to plant crops next year and got about 15 quintals. I got only 6 quintals the following year however. I coped by selling wood that year...... I sold my ox for 500 birr and sold some grain to buy 2 bulls. They grew into mature oxen in a year and I began to use them to plow my land. I also sold some charcoal to buy a calf for 90 birr. When it became a mature ox, I sold it to buy a cow which gave us 4 calves over the following years, one of which died. I also sold one of the oxen to buy a cow.*

> *I now have 2 oxen, 2 cows and 2 calves..... I have sharecropped-in land for the past 5 years, getting 2.5 quintals from it.....We sell goats and ration food to make ends meet. My wife also sold a type of wood called weyeba, that women burn to warm and perfume themselves. My brother helps me every now and then by giving me 50 kilos of grain a year.*

In order to cope with fluctuating crop performance and maintain his assets, Nurtoyar has diversified his income sources by selling wood and charcoal. In addition, he has pursued agricultural strategies by sharecropping land and selling livestock to purchase inputs. His adept management of livestock transactions in which he was able to balance an optimum number of reproductive and draft animals enabled him to increase his livestock holdings under difficult circumstances. He has also engaged in food rationing and accepted gifts of grain from his brother to cope with food insecurity. Nurtoyar's ability to make use of a variety of mechanisms, which was dependent on the specific attributes of his household such as the presence of adequate labor and certain skills, was critical in avoiding destitution.

While there are a number of households who successfully avoid destitution in the face of multiple threats to their livelihoods, others who are unable to do so take up strategies that are peculiar to destitute households. Many destitute households are forced to rent out their land for lack of oxen and other inputs, an option which they may supplement with other income-generating activities. A typical case was that of Muhaili, who had gone to the resettlement areas as discussed above, and remained destitute when he returned.

I came back with 50 birr which I used to buy a calf. The people who had been cultivating my father's land in our absence were going to release the land to us the following year. Till then, I worked as a servant, earning 3.5 quintals of maize. The following year, my relatives plowed some of my land for me while I sharecropped out the rest for lack of oxen. Only part of the land is fertile. I got 2.5 quintals from the sharecropping arrangement and 5.5 quintals from the rest. I was not able to acquire more livestock that year because our grain output did not exceed my family's needs which had grown to a size of four......[These days] our annual grain output fluctuates from 3 to 6 quintals. When we produce less, I sell charcoal and borrow money from traders and farmers, making a payment of 50 kilos of teff and 100 kilos of sorghum for a loan of 60 birr. .... I have also leased out a third of our landholdings for two years because we run out of food. We have been hurt by this. I am eager to get our land back and I will not rent it out again.....The lack of oxen [which is forcing us to rent out our land] is the main constraint that we face. Otherwise, my total landholdings would have been enough for my needs. I have been working in EGS with Concern for about 4-5 years, receiving up to 1.5 quintals of grain a year.

As in the case of many destitute households, Muhaili has responded to the lack of oxen by renting out and sharecropping some of his land, and asking his relatives to plow the rest of his land for him. He has also taken up other strategies typical of destitute households such as farm wage labor, the sale of charcoal, borrowing money at a substantial interest, and working in employment-generating schemes. While such a combination of activities have allowed him to survive, he blames the lack of oxen and the consequent reduced control over his land for his inability to attain a viable livelihood. The strategies that such destitute households undertake, emerging from the lack of productive assets, allow them to live at a subsistence level but often do not permit them to emerge from destitution.

Social Networks and Support of the Destitute

Destitute households who lack the assets necessary for a viable livelihood are commonly dependent on support from their relatives and neighbors for their survival (Yared 1999; 2003). Some of these households face a critical threat to their continued existence when they lose their draft oxen as a result of crop failure. Others may lack the labor required to cultivate their land. One of the most important means by which the destitute receive support therefore is in the form of donations of oxen and labor to have their land plowed. This type of support often comes from close relatives. Damene, who had lost all his livestock due to repeated crop failures, was greatly dependent on this.

Since I did not have any oxen, my brothers and uncles used to do the first plowing for me, and I had it plowed for planting in exchange for straw. I used to join my donkey with my brother's to plow the land also. I have not been able to get my own oxen up to this time. My brothers live close to

16

me and support me by plowing for me. My sister also gives me oxen for 2 to 3 days at a time, as well as 3 cans of teff and 10 cans of barley for seed as a loan, but she usually does not ask me to pay it back after I help her with weeding her fields. Recently, I have been compensating some people who have loaned me some oxen by doing some leatherwork for them.

Damene has been able to receive use different forms of draft power donations from various relatives to cultivate his land, in addition to gifts of grain from his sister. He is not expected to compensate his supporters but he tries to reciprocate by offering them his labor, straw and products of his craft work.

Other households facing a similar dilemma may receive assistance from the general community as well. There is an underlying sense of entitlement that allows such desperate households to claim assistance in draft power for their neighbors. Muhaili, who we saw had lost his oxen due to drought and had returned from the locality that he had been resettled, was continually dependent on his neighbors for draft power. Again, he also attempts to compensate his supporters by giving them animal feed and grazing space.

The following year, my relatives plowed some of my land for me while I sharecropped out the rest for lack of oxen....I continued to beg relatives and neighbors – up to 20 people per year – to have my land plowed, and to sharecrop out a third of the land for 2 years. In return, I assist them by digging for them on their land when they ask for it..... I sell the sorghum stalks for 50 to 80 birr to farmers and also give some to people who plow my land for me ..... I also gave grazing land to others who help me with oxen and grain loans.

The social networks that give rise to such forms of support for needy households are based on various resource exchanges and local institutions that are part of everyday peasant life (Berry 1989: 1993). Most households in a community engage in labor sharing arrangements for various types of agricultural activities. In addition to their economic function, these types of arrangements are a form of social interaction that is a part of membership in the community. As Tadele, an elderly farmer, put it "Most people in the community help each other out if they can [in agricultural tasks], except people who do not get along with anybody. I work together with neighbors and friends." Similarly, Abebaw said "much of our agricultural work is done collectively, in turns. If my friend is working alone, I will join him to work together."

In addition, most households are members of religious associations such as *maheber* and *senbete* which can be the bases of various types of mutual assistance, or of burial associations which can help households take care of potentially costly and impoverishing funerals. The destitute may be unable to participate in the former because they are unable to prepare the feasts required which may have a restricting effect on their social networks, while most households are members of the latter. The statements of Alemnesh, a middle-aged female head of household, regarding her participation in such local associations was typical of destitute households, "I drink coffee with my mother's relatives and go to a monthly commemoration of a relative to one of their houses. I am not in a *Senbete*, but I contribute 2 *injera* for funerals."

The church, in which all Christain members of the community are involved in the form of religious worship and contributions, can be a valuable source of credit for households facing food and cash shortages. Wondimu, a young farmer, stated:

> *When I fell short of grain last Kiremt, I borrowed 50 birr from the church to return it in November with a ten birr interest (20% interest in 5 months). I borrow this much cash from the church every year as do other people. The funds come from the contributions we make to the church.*

The other manner in which both destitute households and those facing temporary difficulties receive critical support is through the grain and cash loans and gifts from community members. Nowadays, this sort of support is usually available only from close relatives. Damene's loans of grain from his sister when he fell short of food, which often became gifts before he could repay them were an example of the sort of assistance that destitute people received. Households in specially unique circumstances such as those just returning from resettlement and in need of assistance in getting back on their feet seemed to have stronger claims on loans of grain or cash as well as draft power. This occurred in the case of Ali Muhe, a middle-aged farmer, who returned penniless from the region in which he and his family had been resettled. He stated "We came back with nothing however, and started to plow some of the poor land that I had inherited – about 7 timad. Our relatives – brothers, uncles – helped us for a year by giving us grain." The initial support he received was critical in enabling him to survive the year he returned and to eventually form a viable household.

Generally, the possibility of getting such loans and gifts was very limited for most households however, especially in comparison to previous days. The deteriorating crop and economic conditions have significantly reduced the scope for mutual support among community members. Mohammed, a young farmer who was short of land, lacked draft power and often food-insecure as a result, had this to say: "I have been able to borrow 60 birr from a cousin in the pre-harvest months of some years to repay it with 50 kgs of sorghum including interest. There is no one else who can lend me money or grain, because people are no longer willing to do so." Similarly, Alemnesh, a middle aged divorcee, who had minimal amounts of land, no other assets and who was often short of food, said "Nobody helps me with loans or anything else. I struggle by myself."

On the other hand, donations of grain resembling charity appeared to persist especially in certain contexts such as the post-harvest season. These could alleviate the food shortages of households who could go as far as begging for food. Shambel, a young man who was a member of a destitute and highly food-insecure household, described how his household resorted to this option.

> *The children from my household stand on the threshing grounds of other people in the community and beg for grain that they will use to purchase*

clothes and receive about 20-30 kgs of grain in total. We tell them to go to certain people. We eat the food they bring and buy them clothes from the sale of goats.

However, this was certainly a last resort for most households, as their sense of pride and dignity prevented them opting for it. Even the children of Shambel's household partly disguised the purpose of their begging by claiming that they would be using it to buy clothes instead of consuming it. In this regard, Amemoye, the old and destitute widow mentioned above, and who had no source of income for food except the employment project, support from her poor son and some farm labor, said, "We have never gone begging people for food because we the people of Wello do not humiliate ourselves. I don't want people to say that my son does not support his mother."

Another way in which people who are down and out are helped out is by being allowed to join a household of a close family member, and contribute to the latter while deriving sustenance from it. This occurred in the case of Beyu, an old divorcee who became destitute after she divorced two husbands. She joined the household of her sister after each of her two divorces. Although her sister was poor herself, they were able to fare better by pooling their labor and income.

I had four children who all died, so [my husband] left me without leaving me anything. I then began to live with my sister. I have had a bad leg since I was a child so I was not able to remarry for another 5 years. I then married an elderly man who had only 3 timad of land which we sharecropped out. We remained in poverty so we got divorced. I therefore started to live with my sister again. We survived the 1984/85 famine together. She would hire out as a farm wage laborer, and collect some wild plants such as Alma, Zenfoq wood and Yewof teff which we ground into a flour to bake a sort of bread. Nobody helped us since most people had left us. Others were trying to survive like we were..... After the famine, we made and sold charcoal and rope. I also used to do threadwork and hair dressing but the former is no longer in demand and women do not come for the latter anymore because I am too old. We were also prevented from selling charcoal about ten years ago, which I used to collect and sell every week.

Although networks of mutual assistance in rural communities are on the decline, those households who have access to remittances or support from more prosperous urban kin are in a much better position to combat destitution or even escape it if they had sunk into destitution in the first place. Mohammed, a young parent who was still living with his father, described how the assistance he received from urban relatives helped them cope with crop failure and eventually regain their asset base.

When our crops failed in 1984/85, we remained in the area, selling our cattle, sheep and goats for food. We sold two oxen whereas two of our oxen, 2 cows, 4 goats and 4 sheep died. Our cousins who used to live in

19

Addis also helped us out by sending money.......My cousin sent us 600 Birr to buy 1 ox for his mother and 1 ox for ourselves. In return, we plowed for her. We had a good harvest in 1987, so we bought a cow which gave birth to six animals subsequently.

Escaping Destitution

Although destitution is a real threat and a common outcome for a significant number of households, many of them who have experienced destitution due to various natural and social causes manage to emerge from it and form viable livelihoods. The possibilities of escaping destitution depend on the strategies pursued by different households, the assets that they are able to access and the general conditions that they face while attempting to reconstruct a livelihood (Devereux, Sharp and Yared 2002; Yared 2002).

The extent to which destitute households can invest and attain success in agriculture is an important determinant of their ability to escape destitution. This is because agriculture is the most significant source of the surplus that can be invested in assets in the context of the rural economy that households find themselves in. This is exemplified in the case of Ali, who had experienced crop failure and subsequent resettlement in Asosa, but returned and later regained his assets by combining his savings from Asosa and the surplus from his agricultural activities. His access to an important productive asset in the form of the land that he had inherited was a necessary element of his capacity to emerge from destitution.

I had brought 150 birr from Asosa which I used to buy two goats. I bought an ox subsequently after selling grain and the 2 goats, and purchased an ox and a heifer in the following years. We thus escaped poverty with the help of my relatives. I now have 2 oxen, 1 cow and 2 calves.

The mixed farming system also provides substantial scope for mutual reinvestment among the different sectors within it. Thus, while crop production allows the investment of surplus grain in livestock assets, some households such as that of Mohammed Yassin, are able to use the cash from livestock sales to rent-in land and expand their grain supply as well. The cow that he owned was the critical asset that enabled him to accumulate and enhance his productivity.

We had a good harvest in 1987, so we bought a cow which gave birth to six animals subsequently. We are now left with three of them after having sold the rest to pay the rent on land that we have been contracting in the past 6 years. The rent has been as much as 650 Birr to rent one timad for 3 years. It is a good piece of land that we plant with sorghum, oats, wheat and teff.

As we saw in the case of Nurtoyar above, the ability to sharecrop or rent-in land is an important means of enhancing one's access to land and productivity and therefore one' assets. A prerequisite for the ability of Nurtoyar's and other similar households' ability to utilize such land transactions to construct a livelihood was their access to their own land and oxen in the first place.

In addition to their access to assets, the success of households in using production strategies to escape from destitution also depends on various conditions that they face in the local context. Crop performance is probably the most important factor that determines whether households can escape destitution or not. Farmers such as Ali, Mohammed Yassin and Nurtoyar were able to make economic progress in years in which they produced surplus grain which they could invest in livestock. The other condition affecting the success of household production strategies is the availability of land on the market and the terms or transactions which can vary in different localities. Mohammed Yassin and Hussein (see below) were able to find a substantial amount of land on the market that they could use to expand their grain supply and income. The relative balance between sharecropping and cash rentals in the local land market also provides varying access to different households in that households with limited access to cash are less able to access land from the latter type of land transaction.

The other means by which some households escape destitution is by diversifying their livelihoods either within or outside of agriculture into such activities as farm labor, migrant labor, grain or livestock trading and construction work. The story of Hussien, who had returned from resettlement to experience steady upward economic mobility over a period of time indicate the role of income diversification, in his case engaging in farm and migrant wage labor, in allowing households to invest in assets. We are also able to see the impact of his extensive involvement in land transactions in reinforcing his productive and investment capacity. The fact that he had the labor capacity was of course an important prerequisite for his ability to engage in such activities.

> *I stayed there for a year and came back by myself when I was in my twenties. I got employment as a plowman in a household for a salary of 200 birr and 1 quintal of grain a year. But I quarreled with him after 4 months and left to stay with relatives, selling charcoal to gain income. I then went to Asayita in place of someone drafted to harvest cotton who paid me 40 birr. I stayed there for 2 months and returned with 200 birr. I bought 2 bulls for 130 birr each while I stayed with relatives. I then hired out as a farmer near Harbu for 35 birr per month for 4 months. I also went to Asayita again to earn enough income to buy a 3rd bull.*

> *I then began to stay with an aunt, plowing her farm in exchange for half of the output which amounted to about 8 quintals..... I have been sharecropping-in as much as 15 to 20 timad, getting up to 10 to 15 quintals from it per year. The land in our area is generally not very productive, so we are able to get some grain only by cultivating a large amount of land. I have also started to rent in land for cash for the past three years. For instance, I rented-in land from Muhaili paying him 490 birr for three years, and 600 birr to rent-in land for eight years from a*

*farmer who does not have oxen. I sell grain as well as goats to pay the
rent on the land and other needs.*

Other households are able to diversify into the non-agricultural sector to achieve the same
results. For instance, Mohammed Yiman, whose parental household had been displaced
by crop failure in 1984/85, used his earnings from his work in construction as a migrant
laborer, to make his initial investment on which he was able to build upon by using
surplus from his agricultural activities. His access to his father's land and his labor were
important bases for the strategies that he used to escape destitution.

> *Pests destroyed what we planted in 1984/85. I left for Wellega, whereas
> the rest of my family were taken to Asosa (resettlement areas). I worked
> in construction for 10 months and came back here where I stayed with
> relatives. I bought a bull with some money I brought from Wellega and
> began to plow my father's land. I subsequently bought a second bull, one
> calf and a goat. I used to produce as much as 15 quintals a year. In the
> following years, I also bought another bull and a goat as well.*

The support that destitute households derive from their social networks can be another
important means by which they escape destitution. The assistance that these households
get in the form of grain or cash loans or donations of oxen and labor can help them meet
their immediate deficits and enable them to resume the productive activities that can put
them back on their feet again. Ali's case, discussed above, demonstrates the critical role
of the support he received from his relatives in grain and draft power after his return from
resettlement in allowing him to reconstruct a livelihood. He acknowledged the initial and
continuing assistance that he got from his relatives by saying, "We thus escaped poverty
with the help of my relatives. I now have 2 oxen, 1 cow and 2 calves. We married-off 3
daughters since we returned from Asosa with the help of our relatives who contributed
money, clothing and grain."

In a related manner, households experiencing events that threaten to throw them into
destitution can fight it off by resorting to relationships of mutual support in the
community. Abebaw, whose productivity was greatly reduced as a result of a land
redistribution that reduced his landholdings, was able to diversify into trading and still
maintain his asset base partly due to the assistance that he received from the community.
His case shows that particularly more cohesive communities such as the one he lived in
have a greater potential for providing the sort of mutual support that can help households
avoid destitution.

> *During the land redistribution of 1990/91 (by the EPRDF), my
> landholdings were reduced from 4 timad to 2.5 timad of infertile land. I
> stopped sharecropping land because the plots were too small. I used to
> produce 20 to 30 quintals before the land redistribution, which declined to
> 10 quintals on average since. I started to neglect farming because I was
> no longer able to produce enough for the family, and got involved in
> trading salt from Mekele. We had to start buying grain from animal sales*

and trading..... We ourselves have asked for help from others, such as when we asked for cash to buy clothes last year and grain in 1990 after the land redistribution. We are able to request loans from many people in Adi Maya, where most people are related to each other.

The Impact of Development Interventions

There are a number of development interventions being carried out by governmental and non-governmental organizations in most localities of the region. Probably the most widespread interventions are the food for work and employment generation schemes. The primary objective of the former is the implementation of development projects while the latter is mainly aimed at providing resources to households facing emergency food shortages while involving them in various development projects. These are carried out in almost all *kebeles* in the region, involving a varying proportion of households from year to year. Although limited in the amount of food and income they provide to participating households, the schemes have come to play an important role in helping many households meet the cash and grain deficits they sustain every year. For instance, Muhaili, who we saw was regularly experiencing food shortages, stated, "I have been working in EGS with CONCERN for about 4-5 years, receiving up to 1.5 quintals of grain a year."

Owing to the limited funds available for disbursal, such schemes often do not go beyond supplementing the food supply of households to allow them to build assets. Moreover, the occurrence of corrupt practices sometimes prevents poorer households from benefiting. In this regard, Abebaw stated the following about officials in his kebele, where for the past year ordinarily transparent means of selecting beneficiaries appear to have been abandoned:

> *There is also quite a bit of favoritism and corruption in who gets to benefit from such programs. Officials register people but then ignore the list to benefit people they favor. The poor have not benefited, while the friends of officials get assistance. Most people are uneducated, so that they cannot appeal against unfairness and injustice. Much of the aid that comes is therefore taken by officials.*

The other significant intervention in the region is the credit provided by various agencies to allow households to acquire seed, breed and fatten animals and to engage in various income-generating activities such as trading. This has often been quite beneficial to households, although its success is often constrained by such factors as drought, animal deaths or low demand for commodities. One of the most beneficial loans is the one meant for the purchase of seed, the shortages of which often severely inhibits the productive potential of households and threaten their viability. Thus, Damene, who regularly faced food and cash shortages due to land shortages and natural causes, stated "I also borrowed money for some teff seed about three years ago which gave us a good yield, but they have not asked us to repay it."

Although, credit schemes have significant potential in enabling households to invest in various assets and productive activities, their impact is weakened by a number of factors. One of these is the low supply of credit in relation to the demand for it. Only a few households per kebele are able to get credit every year, leaving out many households who would like to have it. Loans for acquiring animals for fattening or breeding purposes are especially in high but unsatisfied demand. The other constraint on credit schemes is the reluctance of farmers to take loans which arises from their fear that they may not be successful in the projects that the loans would be used for, thereby falling into debt as a result. The sentiments of Mohammed Yimer are held by many poor households.

> *I have not applied for a livestock or seed loan because I may not be able to repay it. They have been encouraging us to borrow seeds of sorghum, teff and chickpeas, but I have refused to take any. Others have been taking loans, but have been experiencing crop failures and selling grain to repay it. Our land is not appropriate for inputs because it is very sloppy.*

The use of loans to purchase inputs was especially likely to fail as a result of poor crop performance due to drought, pests or other factors. This was the case with Tadele, an old and destitute farmer, who became indebted as a result. He was also unable to repay the loan which he used to buy an ox, therefore having to sell it.

> *I got 86 Birr worth of fertilizer on credit and 3 kgs of teff for free. But the output was unsatisfactory and I am going to have to sell some grain to repay my debt. I also got credit to buy an ox (from a program directed at households with no oxen), but had to sell it when my stock of lentils - which I meant to use to repay my loan - was stolen.*

Problems with the implementation of loans such as delays in their disbursal as well as their short term nature also sometimes prevented their effectiveness. In this respect, Nurtoyar said, "I also got a loan of 12.5 birr for seed quite late, so I just used it to buy grain for food and repaid the loan later." Although he benefited from the loan in terms of acquiring food, the intended support for his productivity and food security was not realized.

The construction of roads has led to improvements in prices and availability of grain and commodities that has had a measurablly positive impact on the welfare of households. The related growth in urban centers has also enhanced employment opportunities as well. The statements of Abebaw clearly describe this process:

> *The construction of the road from Lalibela to Sekota three years ago has brought about lower grain and cloth prices. Prices have declined from about 3 birr to 2 birr for wheat, and from 5 birr to 3 birr for teff. Clothes used to be available only in shops which were mainly accessible for the wealthy, but now clothes are available in market stalls for 3, 5 or 10 birr each. The road that was built from Tigray to Sekota has made more salt available on the market, but it has not been as beneficial. Sekota has been*

growing significantly in recent years. We can find commodities such as kerosene, berbere and sugar, that we were not able to get earlier.

Similarly, Moges recognized the impact of that same road not only on grain prices but also on their availability, as well as on the growth in the size and employment opportunities in the town.

Cheap grains like sorghum are now available at Sekota since the road from Lalibela to Sekota was constructed. This, in addition to the construction of the hospital, has led to the growth of Sekota. A lot of private houses are now being built, which has created work for us.

Conclusion

The case studies brought out the different experiences of households with respect to destitution, including those that had undergone, avoided, coped with and escaped destitution. This has brought out the nature and causes of destitution, and the role of livelihood strategies and social support networks in dealing with processes of destitution.

We have seen that the most common way by which households became destitute was after they experienced severe or repeated crop failure due to drought or other natural causes which led to the sale or death of their livestock assets. This was a relatively rapid form of becoming destitute, although in the case of some more resilient households, this outcome occurs only with the impact of repeated crop failures. Some of these households are often forced to take up strategies such as renting out land or taking usurious loans that compound their state of destitution.

Other households appear fated for destitution because they had very poor access to key productive resources such as land, oxen and sometimes labour from the time they were formed. Events in the social development of households can also push some households towards destitution. The most common way this happens is when women lose their husbands due to divorce or death and are forced to lead households without critical male labour or management skills. Recently-formed households who have missed the last local land redistribution and who may have received a very small marriage endowment in terms of assets from their parents, as well as the elderly who lack labour and may have passed on much of their land and livestock when marrying-off their children, are also vulnerable to destitution processes.

While most households experience severe crises such as the occurrence of droughts or pests, debilitating illness or deaths, not all of them are reduced to destitution. Despite coming under severe stress and even sustaining substantial asset loss, more resilient households manage to avoid total destitution because their initially strong asset base allows them to retain some of it after the crises. Other households succeed in avoiding destitution despite shortfalls in their agricultural production by diversifying their income sources. Access to assets and skills that are prerequisites to diversification is critical in order for one to successfully combine agricultural and non-agricultural strategies in order to avoid destitution. For many households, their social networks in the community are a critical source of support that can act as a safety net.

As a result of some of the processes mentioned above, many households are reduced to extended states of destitution. Such households are then forced to take up strategies that enable them to survive as destitutes. These strategies are often either compromising or are coping mechanisms that do not allow such households to emerge from destitution. Resort to income earning activities such as farm or off-farm employment, food-for-work, wood or charcoals sales or loan requests are ways that destitute households cope with food and income shortages, although such sources of income are too small to allow households to acquire the assets that would allow them to escape destitution. Networks of social support are vital to the survival of destitute households. Since many destitute households lack the labour and draft power that they need to maintain a minimum level of agricultural productivity, donations of these inputs from the community enable them to survive because they can produce food without having to rent out all or some of their land. In addition, some people who are so destitute that they have no possibility of living on their own may be allowed to join the households of close family members, deriving sustenance from the latter while contributing with their labour.

Having become destitute, there are some households who escape destitution to regain their livelihoods. One of the ways such households achieve this is by investing in agriculture and using surplus to rebuild their assets. Other households are able to rebuild their asset base in a sustained fashion by combining surplus from crop and livestock production to enhance their assets and productivity in each sector. These strategies also require sufficient access to land and labour as well as favourable crop performance if they are to be successful. There are households that escape destitution by successfully resorting to both farm and non-farm activity to gain the resources that they can invest in assets. This type of strategy requires a substantial amount of skill and labour. Households that have succeeded in escaping destitution have also often been beneficiaries of a helping hand from their kin or friends in the local community or from urban areas that has allowed them to 'get back on their feet'.

Preventing and Reducing Destitution

In order to stop and reverse growing levels of impoverishment and destitution in an effective and sustainable manner, it is imperative that we address their root causes – drought and others causes of crop failure, low productivity, lack of assets, weak markets and non-agricultural sector, and overpopulation. This requires us to come up with focussed and coherent strategies which allow us to engage these problems in a comprehensive and multi-pronged fashion. The following four strategies should all be integral components of an overall anti-poverty effort. These are an anti-drought/famine strategy, a production strategy, an income diversification strategy and a demographic strategy.

1. An anti-drought/famine strategy

Droughts and other causes of crop failure are responsible for causing massive asset loss and destitution in the highlands of Ethiopia. The timely provision of food aid before people begin to dispose of their assets in order to purchase food, that would be made possible through improved early warning mechanisms and consolidation of grain reserves at national, regional and local levels, should therefore be an important goal. Given the failure to provide timely and adequate relief and the reduction in animal feed that forces households to sell-off their livestock, the potential of livestock purchase schemes for regional, national or international markets needs to be explored. Programs directed at post-drought recovery such as assistance and credit for acquiring seed, draft power, and reproductive animals need to be strengthened. Insurance schemes set up through cooperatives in which regular contributions by households can be matched by funds from external sources that together can be withdrawn in times of crises can become a beneficial and desirable source of security. Other vital components of an anti-drought strategy are strengthened nutritional supplementation programs for malnourished children, health interventions and school feeding. Efforts to make agriculture less dependent on rainfall through local water storage mechanisms and irrigation are important as well.

2. An agricultural strategy

Low agricultural productivity due to lack of assets and technology, unfavourable ecology and resource degradation, is another significant structural factor behind growing destitution and poverty. Again, substantial attention to water storage and irrigation in addition to the promotion of integrated pest management can play a vital role in stabilizing and enhancing productivity. For localities and households that can optimally adopt them, agricultural inputs and improved animal breeds in addition to expanded veterinary services will continue to be important basis for expanding production. If we are to motivate farmers to invest in conserving and enhancing the productivity of their landholdings, tenure security has to be strengthened by undertaking an emphatic and convincing step towards the institution of permanent land rights through land registrations and public awareness efforts. This will be linked to efforts to expand tree planting and the availability of fuel wood. A conscious strategy to promote the emergence of well-to-do farmers, in contrast to previous state policy aimed at levelling rural society, by promoting the unconstrained exchange of land through rental arrangements and support in terms of technology and credit provision, is indispensable if we are to achieve sustained growth in agricultural productivity and marketed surplus.

3. An income diversification strategy

The inexorable decline in the size and productivity of landholdings as well as the unfavourable climatic conditions that has made agriculture an increasingly unreliable bases for rural livelihoods calls for concerted efforts to diversify the income sources of farmers in order to reduce their vulnerability and to enhance their ability to invest in assets. Poor and destitute household are in especially high need of income diversification interventions. Given the small size of the non-agricultural sector in rural areas, one of the realistic ways of achieving this is through employment-creation schemes that will supplement currently on-going safety nets. This requires more focussed targeting of poor or destitute households and payments substantial enough to allow accumulation and economic mobility. Priority should be given to employment projects that will sustainably enhance local employment such as irrigation, roads and construction. In contrast to previous programs, attention should be given to the quality of outputs and to imparting skills that participants can market. Destitutes who are unable to work such as the elderly and the disabled should continue to get food aid.

The other means by which households' resilience and ability to build-up assets can be strengthened is by considerably expanding the provision of credit so as to meet the substantial unmet demand for it. Options with respect to type of loan available to different types of households in terms of size, type and repayment schedule should be maintained to allow households to meet their different needs, e.g. access to draft power for oxen-less households and diversification towards self-employment or access to reproductive animals or poultry for land-short and female-headed households. Credit schemes should be increasingly integrated with saving schemes in order to support asset accumulation, to move towards insuring clients against production and income shortfalls, and to address possibilities of and concerns about indebtedness due to failed credit financed projects through strengthened linkages with safety-net programs. Integration of such schemes with training for self or wage employment as well as the introduction of cooperative marketing for peasant products is also highly desirable. Indeed, there is a significant need for the expansion of training programs, the scale and types of which need to be informed by market demand on a continual basis.

The integration and diversification of local and regional economies probably provides the best potential for availing the increased income-earning opportunities and market access that will have the greatest impact on destitution. Sustained attention to the expansion of rural road networks and transportation, support for the growth of markets and urban centers by encouraging construction and development of infrastructure including power, promoting the development of the service sector and tourism, can help us achieve these results. In the same spirit, continued attention to the expansion of primary education will allow young people, including the children of the destitute, to take advantage of the new opportunities that will open up.

4. A demographic strategy

Increasing poverty is to some extent a function of growing population, which has resulted in diminishing farm sizes and associated resource degradation. A sustainable strategy aimed at poverty reduction in the North-Eastern highlands therefore, needs to reduce the person/land ratio by facilitating population movement from the region into other locations and economic sectors. One of the ways this can be attained is by expanding the scope for short and long term labour migration by promoting the growth of commercial farms and surplus producing farms in favourable regions. The institution of permanent land-rights will be indispensable in promoting the mobility of rural people by reducing the need to remain tied to their landholdings in order to retain access to them. The potential of voluntary resettlement is something that should be explored in a cautious and well-planned fashion, involving adequate studies of the ecological suitability of target areas, and the provision of adequate amounts of land, productive capital, infrastructure and health care to a limited number of re-settlers in the short term to enable them to attain viable livelihoods and the surplus production that can be a source of grain supplies and employment for food-deficit and poorer regions. The possible role of planned resettlement as a valve for reducing population pressure should only be a long-term objective. A conscious strategy to permit small and large urban centers to attain faster growth by encouraging investment and infra-structural development and expanding education and training should be used as another means of reducing population pressure in the rural areas. Urgent efforts directed at expanding access to family planning methods and reducing the incidence of early marriage will enable households to better manage and reduce their fertility, also contributing to a more balanced rate of population growth to occur.

References

Aklilu Kidanu and Dessalegn Rahmato 2000. *Listening to the Poor: A Study Based on Selected Rural and Urban Sites in Ethiopia.* Discussion Paper No. 3. Addis Ababa, Forum for Social Studies.

Dasgupta, P. 1993. *An Inquiry into Well-Being and Desitution.* Oxford: Clarendon Press.

Dessalegn Rahmato 1991. *Famine and Survival Strategies.* Uppsala: The Scandinavian Institute of African Studies.

Dessalegn Rahmato 2002. "*Poverty and Agricultural Involution in Ethiopia*" in Dessalegn Rahmato (ed.) *Some Aspects of Poverty in Ethiopia: Three Selected Papers.* Addis Ababa, Forum for Social Studies.

Devereux, S., Sharp, K. and Yared Amare 2002. *Destitution in the Northeastern Highlands* (Amhara National Regional State). Institute of Development Studies, University of Sussex and Save the Children-UK Ethiopia.

Ellis, F. 2000. *Rural Livelihoods and Diversity in Developing Countries.* Oxford: Oxford University Press.

Goyder H. and Catherine Goyder. 1988 "Case Studies of Famine: Ethiopia." pp. 73-110 in Donald Curtis, Michael Hubbard and Andrew Shepherd (eds.) *Preventing Famine. Policies and Prospects for Africa,* New York: Routledge.

McCann, J. 1987. "The Social Impact of Drought in Ethiopia: Oxen, Households, and Some Implications for Rehabilitation." In *Drought and Hunger in Africa: Denying Famine a Future.* Michael H. Glantz, ed. Cambridge: Cambridge University Press, pp. 245-67.

MEDAC 1999. *Poverty Situation in Ethiopia.* Welfare Monitoring Unit, Ministry of Economic Development and Cooperation, Addis Ababa.

Swift, J. 1989. Why Are Rural People Vulnerable to Famine? *IDS Bulletin* Vol.20, No. 2.

Walker, P. 1989. *Famine Early Warning Systems: Victims and Destitution.* London: Earthscan.

Webb, P., Joachim Von Braun and Yisehac Yohannes 1992. *Famine in Ethiopia: Policy Implications of Coping Failure at National and Household Levels.* Research Report 92. International Food Policy Research Institute, Washington, D.C.

Yared Amare 1999. *Household Resources, Strategies and Food Security. A Study of Amhara Households in Wogda, Northern Shewa.* Addis Ababa: Addis Ababa, University Press.

Yared Amare 2002. *Rural Poverty in Ethiopia. Household Case Studies from North Shewa.* Forum for Social Studies Discussion Paper No. 9. Addis Ababa:

Yared Amare 2003. "Socio-Economic Dimensions of Rural Poverty in Ethiopia. A Qualitative Study of Two Communities in Northern Shewa." *Journal of Ethiopian Studies* 2003 (Forthcoming).

Annex

Socio-economic Profile of Case Households

Name of Hhhd	Sex of Hhhd	Age of Hhhd	Family Size	Land - holdings	Labor Status[2]	Oxen No	Poverty Status
Abebaw	M	43	8	2.5 timad, ~5 rented in	Good	2	Middle Income
Alemnesh	F	40	1	3 timad, rented out	Poor	0	Destitute
Ali	M	51	6	7 timad	Adequate	2	Middle Income
Amemoye	F	60	2	0 timad	Poor	0	Destitute
Beyu	F	70	1	0 timad	Poor	0	Destitute
Damene	M	58	7	3.5 timad, 2.5 rented out	Adequate	0	Poor
Hussein	M	38	5	3 timad, 15-20 rented in	Adequate	2	Well-off
Moges	M	48	7	4 timad	Adequate	2	Poor
Mohammed Seid	M	32	4	2 timad, 2 rented in	Adequate	1	Poor
Mohmmed Yassin	M	30	3	2 timad, 1 rented in	Adequate	1	Poor
Mohammed Yiman	M	40	3	1 timad, 4 rented in	Adequate	2	Well-off
Mohammed Yimer	M	37	5	2 timad, 2 rented in	Adequate	0	Destitute
Muhaili	M	45	8	~4 timad, 1.5 rented out	Good	0	Destitute
Nurtoyar	M	48	6	6 timad	Good	1	Poor
Shambel	Son of HHHd	24	9	.75 timad	Good	0	Destitute
Tadele	M	60	1	2 timad	Poor	0	Destitute
Wondimu	M	~30	3	2 timad	Adequate	1	Poor
Zenitu	F	40	4	1.5 timad	Poor	2	Middle Income

Notes: [s] Shola meda *kebele,* [y] Yezaba *kebele.*

[2] Labor status: Good – More than 2 adult laborers; Adequate – At least 1 male labor and 1 female labor, Poor – Lacking at least 1 male or female labor.

FSS PUBLICATIONS LIST

FSS Newsletter

Medrek, now renamed BULLETIN (Quarterly since 1998. English and Amharic)

FSS Discussion Papers

No. 1. *Water Resource Development in Ethiopia: Issues of Sustainability and Participation.* Dessalegn Rahmato. June 1999

No. 2. *The City of Addis Ababa: Policy Options for the Governance and Management of a City with Multiple Identity.* Meheret Ayenew. December 1999

No. 3. *Listening to the Poor: A Study Based on Selected Rural and Urban Sites in Ethiopia.* Aklilu Kidanu and Dessalegn Rahmato. May 2000

No. 4. *Small-Scale Irrigation and Household Food Security. A Case Study from Central Ethiopia.* Fuad Adem. February 2001

No. 5. *Land Redistribution and Female-Headed Households.* By Yigremew Adal. November 2001

No. 6. *Environmental Impact of Development Policies in Peripheral Areas: The Case of Metekel, Northwest Ethiopia.* Wolde-Selassie Abbute. Forthcoming, 2001

No. 7. *The Environmental Impact of Small-scale Irrigation: A Case Study.* Fuad Adem. Forthcoming, 2001

No. 8. *Livelihood Insecurity Among Urban Households in Ethiopia.* Dessalegn Rahmato and Aklilu Kidanu. October 2002

No. 9. *Rural Poverty in Ethiopia: Household Case Studies from North Shewa.* Yared Amare. December 2002

No.10. *Rural Lands in Ethiopia: Issues, Evidences and Policy Response.* Tesfaye Teklu. May 2003

No.11. *Resettlement in Ethiopia: The Tragedy of Population Relocation in the 1980s.* Dessalegn Rahmato. June 2003

FSS Monograph Series

No. 1. *Survey of the Private Press in Ethiopia: 1991-1999.* Shimelis Bonsa. 2000

No. 2. *Environmental Change and State Policy in Ethiopia*: *Lessons from Past Experience.* Dessalegn Rahmato. 2001

FSS Conference Proceedings

1. *Issues in Rural Development. Proceedings of the Inaugural Workshop of the Forum for Social Studies, 18 September 1998.* Edited by Zenebework Taddesse. 2000

2. *Development and Public Access to Information in Ethiopia.* Edited by Zenebework Tadesse. 2000

3. *Environment and Development in Ethiopia.* Edited by Zenebework Tadesse. 2001

4. *Food Security and Sustainable Livelihoods in Ethiopia.* Edited by Yared Amare. 2001

5. *Natural Resource Management in Ethiopia.* Edited by Alula Pankhurst. 2001

6. *Poverty and Poverty Policy in Ethiopia.* Special issue containing the papers of FSS' final conference on poverty held on 8 March 2002

Consultation Papers on Poverty

No. 1.   *The Social Dimensions of Poverty.* Papers by Minas Hiruy, Abebe Kebede, and Zenebework Tadesse. Edited by Meheret Ayenew. June 2001

No. 2.   *NGOs and Poverty Reduction.* Papers by Fassil W. Mariam, Abowork Haile, Berhanu Geleto, and Jemal Ahmed. Edited by Meheret Ayenew. July 2001

No. 3.   *Civil Society Groups and Poverty Reduction.* Papers by Abonesh H. Mariam, Zena Berhanu, and   Zewdie Shitie. Edited by Meheret Ayenew. August 2001

No. 4.   *Listening to the Poor.* Oral Presentation by Gizachew Haile, Senait Zenawi, Sisay Gessesse and Martha Tadesse. In Amharic. Edited by Meheret Ayenew. November 2001

No.5.   *The Private Sector and Poverty Reduction [Amharic].*   Papers by Teshome Kebede, Mullu Solomon and Hailemeskel Abebe. Edited by Meheret Ayenew, November 2001

No.6.   *Government, Donors and Poverty Reduction.* Papers by H.E. Ato Mekonnen Manyazewal, William James Smith and Jeroen Verheul. Edited by Meheret Ayenew, February 2002.

No.7.   *Poverty and Poverty Policy in Ethiopia.* Edited by Meheret Ayenew, 2002

Books

1.   *Ethiopia: The Challenge of Democracy from Below.* Edited by Bahru Zewde and Siegfried Pausewang. Nordic African Institute, Uppsala and Forum for Social Studies, Addis Ababa. 2002

Special Publications

Thematic Briefings on Natural Resource Management, Enlarged Edition. Edited by Alula Pankhurst. Produced jointly by the Forum for Social Studies and the University of Sussex. January 2001

New Series

• **Gender Policy Dialogue Series**

No. 1   *Gender and Economic Policy.* Edited by Zenebework Tadesse. March 2003
No. 2   *Gender and Poverty (Amharic).* Edited by Zenebework Tadese. March 2003

• **Consultation Papers on Environment**

No. 1   *Environment and Environmental Change in Ethiopia.* Edited by Gedion Asfaw. Consultation Papers on Environment. March 2003

No. 2   *Environment, Poverty and Gender.* Edited by Gedion Asfaw. Consultation Papers on Environment. May 2003

No. 3   *Environmental Conflict.* Edited by Gedion Asfaw. Consultation Papers on Environment. July 2003

No. 4   *Economic Development and Its Environmental Impact.* Edited by Gedion asfaw. Consultation papers on Environment. August, 2003

• **FSS Studies on Poverty**

No. 1   *Some Aspects of Poverty in Ethiopia: Three Selected Papers.* Papers by Dessalegn Rahmato, Meheret Ayenew and Aklilu Kidanu. Edited by Dessalegn Rahmato. March 2003.

No. 2   *Faces of Poverty: Life in Gäta, Wälo.* Harald Aspen. June 2003

No. 3   *Destitution in the North-Eastern Highlands of Ethiopia.* Yared Amare. August, 2003

www.ingramcontent.com/pod-product-compliance
Lightning Source LLC
Chambersburg PA
CBHW080844270326
41929CB00016B/2917